ne

Speak to the Earth

Jean Stevens' poems have appeared in *London Magazine, Stand, The North, Mslexia, Other Poetry, Smoke, Brittle Star, The Frogmore Papers, The High Window* and the *Bridport Prizewinners' Anthology (2016)*, and have been broadcast on BBC Radio 3 and Radio 4. She is a past winner of the Yorkshire Post Poetry Prize and the Leeds Libraries Writing Prize, and was recently shortlisted for the Poetry Business Pamphlet Competition and *The Rialto* Poetry Prize.

Her plays have been performed at Derby Playhouse, the Edinburgh Festival, Harrogate Theatre and West Yorkshire Playhouse, and her stand-up comedy script won the Polo Prize at London's Comedy Store.

As a professional actor she has credits for stage, film and television.

jeanstevenspoet.co.uk

These are searching, restless poems, haunted by both darkness and light, by how we damage the earth and how we are forever connected to it. Their yearning for what is tender within us as well as what is wild is both a surprise and a delight.
Kim Moore

Filmic and beautiful, full of warmth and drama
Kay Mellor OBE

An exciting contemporary voice
Daljit Nagra

Persuasive and deeply moving
The Yorkshire Times

A sure hand
Ian McMillan

Also by Jean Stevens

Poetry

Performances (Pica Press 1999)
Undressing in Winter (Matador 2008)
Beyond Satnav (Indigo Dreams Publishing 2016)
Driving in the Dark (Naked Eye Publishing 2018)

Plays

Twockers, Knockers and Elsie Smith (1997)
Journey (1998)
both published by Smith and Kraus, USA

SPEAK TO THE EARTH

Jean Stevens

Naked Eye Publishing

© Jean Stevens 2019

All rights reserved

Book design and typesetting by Naked Eye

ISBN: 9781910981078

www.nakedeyepublishing.co.uk

Acknowledgements

Some of these poems were first published in *Brittle Star*, *Dream Catcher*, *The Frogmore Papers*, *The High Window*, and *Smoke* magazines. The poem *Madeleine* appeared as part of the 2019 exhibition of poetry and art at the University of Cumbria Festival of Mental Health.

SPEAK TO THE EARTH

Ask now the beasts, and they shall teach thee;
and the fowls of the air, and they shall tell thee:
or speak to the earth, and it shall teach thee.

King James Bible
Job:12,7-8

Contents

I Hunting the Light

And	13
Hunting the light	14
Light	15
Night safari	16
Outback	17
Seasons	18
Day	19
British summer time	20
Lighthouse	21
Back	22
That day	23

II The Edge

The edge	27
Silence	28
Hefted	29
Picture window	30
For three days now	31
Crosby Beach	32
Grange-over-Sands	34
Dolphins	35
Great Barrier Reef	36
Rivers	37
To my visitor	38

III Feral Cat

Feral cat	41
Fashion accessory	42
All I did	43
The lions	44
Overnight	45

Stony lane..46
Under the saddle...47
Crystal horse..48
Presence...49
Unsuitable shoes...50
Drama school...51
Wild..52
The twinning of books..53

IV Speak to the Earth

Garsdale...57
If it happens...58
Put an ear to the ground..59
Gagudju man..60
Madeleine...61
And if, after all...62
Beech tree...63
Kindling..64
Wild rhododendrons...65
In praise of the potato...66
Restless land...67
The path of desire...68

V Legacy

The strangers..71
Gaia writes home..72
Cross-questioning...73
Waking...74
Ice storm...75
The dogs...76
Tyger..77
Palm Cove, Queensland..78
Legacy..79

I

Hunting the Light

And

And the girl stepped out of a cloud
right onto the cinder path and her hair
shone like copper coins placed on the eyes
of the dead and underfoot lay the bones
of the earth, where the roots of the oaks
and the beeches were all beginning
to shift and the clay and the rubble rose up
and a voice came out of the mountain:
What have you done to the earth?

And the boy left the field of ashes
and hurled his heavy Kalashnikov
right into a pit of tar and he had the eyes
of the damned, and the judge and the jury
stood up at the trial of all the nations,
and their voices were those of lions:
What have you done to the children?

And the stars and the planets
fell out of their orbits, the horses
broke their chains and plunged
their hooves through the ground.
There was roar after roar of thunder
round the coiffured heads of state
and not a single coin remained
to buy off the devil's curse:
May you reap what you have sown.

And the horses came out
of the shadows into the light,
along with the girl and the boy,
and behind them with eyes on fire
came one, then two, then three,
then a thousand marching children
and the horses lifted their heads
and flexed their powerful wings.

Hunting the light

Looking for the aurora borealis
we immersed ourselves in Jukkasjärvi
and, snuggled in Lapland clothes,
hurtled through frozen landscapes
behind thirty-two racing legs
then slept in the ice on reindeer skins.

We took a plane to Tromsø,
a boat to Kirkenes, then a coach,
struggling behind a giant plough
through snow piled twelve feet deep,
seeking the Northern Lights, as drifts
closed in and marooned us in the dark.

And, far beyond Reykjavik,
we spent long nights wrapped in fur
and sleepless under the stars.

Three separate years, three journeys,
waiting for those green and violet
surges to ripple across the sky.

Light

Suppose, as Jean-Paul Sartre did, tomorrow's dawn is not a sun. Suppose it's an orange. Then everything will change.

What will change most is light. The quality of light. Light as a quality.

I would like light to be an animal. Perhaps a gazelle. Would we recognise a gazelle or would we apprehend light, only light?

I say only light, but light isn't only. Light is everything.

What if we could see, that is contain, light? If we gathered it, would the rest of the world be dark, or would there be no rest of the world?

Does poetry consist of light, or can we say poetry is the bride of light?

What of the rainbow? White light is not truly white light.

And light both is and is not like waves rippling on a pond. Light both is and is not like streams of particles, tiny drops of water sprayed from a garden hose.

When you went, you took the light with you. You stored it all in your torch and pointed the torch the other way.

The word I've been avoiding has barged in. Is death the absence of light or light that blinds?

When I had the operation to swap the lenses in my eyes, what happened to and in my eyes when there were no lenses? They would be space. They would be black. Going back to the cave. Going back.

Everything is just out of reach. Enlighten me.

Night safari

At the Singapore Night Safari, animals roam freely in moonlight in environments replicating their lives in the wild. Visitors and animals are separated only by the slimmest of man-made divides.

I walked the rainforest's moonlit trail
and found myself among leopards.

They were lean, honed by hunting
and hunger and, as flesh and muscle
ebbed and flowed, I saw
down to the beat of blood
and the almost liquid bone.

Their skin was a print of their own
dark paws walking on sand,
their flanks were brandy and treacle,
brown ale held to the light.

I knelt by the narrow divide
and a leopard lay opposite,
mirrored light in his midnight eyes.

He didn't blink and I was held
till he stretched and showed his claws.
I turned to the man who stood next to me.
We're nothing he said.

Outback

No ambient light,
stars bold against the midnight sky,
but there's not a constellation I know.
Orion hunts elsewhere,
and the Southern Cross
has usurped the Polar Star.

If I stay here, that reliable
guide will never come back,
and if I go walkabout,
a lone pilgrim, nothing
will show me the way.

I'm part of the northern
hills of home, the trees, the grass,
the rain, yet could learn
to be at the Red Centre with heat,
dry soil, acres of open land.
What shakes me

is my lack of connection to the stars
even though I know that
when the earth swings
out of control, humankind
will only have been a minor blip
in light that died ages ago.

Seasons

August in Greece.
I sit in the back seat
and someone else is driving.

It's dusk, warm and humid,
fireflies, crickets,
the fragrance of honeysuckle,
dust in the streets,
half-open windows
throwing squares of light
into the dark.

February in my own country
was stunning cold,
treacherous in drifted snow

for underneath were traps:
smashed fences, gates
torn from their hinges
in relentless gales.

I stumbled my way to April
when the first swoops
and curls across the sky
meant swallows returning

and I thought that
spring might come
in a burst of song.

Day

creeps in without fanfare:
hovering clouds, a few
patches of faded blue,

the outline of trees,
tracery of branches,

uncertain twigs, sprays of leaf,
blackbirds rooting in grass

but no visible rising sun,
no rays of colour,

just enough retreat of the dark
to show it's not night.

I imagine myself being told
to look for the light,

to immerse myself in what's still here
and be glad of the loan.

British summer time

Since the clocks went forward an hour,
when I wake the light falls differently

missing the thinning copse,
slanting between the single beech
and the replying flash
from farmhouse windows,

livening the bedroom wall
as the sun paints a moving calendar

in the mirror and along the stitching
of the old embroidered sampler
then across the new framed poem

where, on a background
you photographed here
of limestone pavements
at Malham Cove, are words
that recall Sydney, Broken Hill,
Kakadu and Arnhem Land

where the light touching your room
will be from the moon.

Lighthouse

Early morning.
The cliff path narrow.
Gulls. A sea fret.

Through the mist
on the horizon,
a ghost
of a boat.

Ahead
the shrouded
lighthouse.

Silence
deepened by the call
of birds.

Our next stop
the far end
of the cliff.

The mist
thickening,
the lighthouse
fading,
and as yet unlit.

Back

To forget the tough climb ahead
I turned and walked back
through the night to the snickets,
the alleyways, the secret dens,
the moors where an eager seven-year-old
first saw a sparrowhawk.

Dawn flashed behind gorse,
light flowed through the hawthorns,
my footprints in damp grass
were small and sure.

I ran freely, flung myself
down on the hill's rise,
watched clouds unravel
as sun took charge of the blue,
my laughter that of a child.

Like wisps of cloud,
a life can unravel too,
and I knew I must return
through too little explored terrain
till I came once more to the dark
start of the hardest climb.

That day

the sun continued to alternate
tiny changes between brightness
and shade, and light washed
across the lake, reflecting
reeds and purple irises,
moorhens, mallards and swans
upside down in the still water.

Mist should have formed like a shroud,
blanked out the life of the waterbirds
and washed away all colour.
Cold rain should have pelted
the lake, shattered its surface,
muddied its deeps, that day,
the day they told me.

II

The Edge

The edge

In the blue hour
something unknown
is there in the space
between twilight and dark,

where tides at the edge of the land
turn from ebb to flow, and where
light begins to withdraw
as summer slips into autumn,

between words
that might carry you
down through grass, soil,
stone, to the centre
from where all language springs

or, after a hairpin bend, lead you
on to a narrow track,
at one side the high unforgiving bank,
on the other that fresh-air drop.

Where a narrow route leads between a high bank and a sheer plunge into a valley, rally drivers sometimes refer to the danger as a 'fresh-air drop'.

Silence

Not like the hush as the champion
serves and we wait for the wave
of raucous release.

Not like the held breath
when actors take us
deep inside ourselves.

Not like the pause
when he looks at you and you know
what he's going to suggest.

Not like the hesitation before
ripping open
that loaded envelope.

Not like the horrified gap
when you've just said
something unforgiveable.

Not like the tension
before anaesthesia
and the scary countdown.

Not like anything else at all,
this fear, this shivering on the edge
of the cliff

when whatever
fills the silence
won't suffice.

Hefted

Hefted : accustomed and attached to an area of upland pasture.

It's cloistered in the depths of the valley
inside this old house, where cellos
have left echoes in the stone,
poets' words are carved in the beams,
and the bones of cattle lie under slate

but one day I will follow the hefted sheep
out of here through clear northern light
to climb the far hills and beyond to where
there are no buildings, no roads, no noise
except the battering of the wind.

Picture window
i.m. G.P. Stevens

A thump against the glazing
troubled the room's suburban calm
and left the glass shivering

and I saw that a young woodpecker
lay hunched on the path outside.
His wings, that moments before
defeated gravity with ease,
looked heavy as stone.

The second one in a month to die
like this, his head bent almost parallel
along the broken neck.

I'd put seeds and nuts in protected places,
stuck flying hawks on the windows,
but still he was gone in a flash.

For three days now

For three days now there have been no birds.
The wrens have gone from the drystone walls,
blackbirds aren't here to scavenge the grass
or the goldfinches to flash their wings.

I never realised how their songs and warnings
ringing across the garden and over the hills
were woven into every moment,
how, when swallows rode the thermals
or starlings spiralled against the sky
they were so much a part of my world.

Seeds and nuts hang untouched,
hollies and mountain ash still have their fruit;
the quiet is painful to the ears
like those cold, empty moments
when you can't believe news of a death.

The hundred years beech was felled at dawn
the river is overflowing
and there are no birds.

Crosby Beach

Silent, rusting men stand round me
and gaze out to sea.
At the corner of my eye
a power station bullies
the shore.

Someone's had fun with the waiting men,
dressed two in Liverpool's red and white,
and a child is looking between
another figure's legs for what he knows
to be the missing bits.

Dogs splash on the edge of the surf,
children scream and laugh,
a man takes off his clothes,
puts on a wetsuit, blacks out his face,
hands and feet, and stands close to his
iron counterpart as his wife takes a photograph.

The kids, the dogs and the granddads
are loving this place
where the wind makes a bird's nest of their hair,

but for each of them there comes a moment
when they, too, look out to sea
and imagine their own Viking ships
or clippers, or Kon-Tikis of long ago.

The water rises slowly
and the standing men are indistinguishable now
from those who can move, and all
are evolved from the fish,

are explorers who, when they sail, might drop
off the ends of the earth,
or are men who take to the sea
to conquer or to die.

Like the urge at the top of a cliff,
something is pulling us all towards water
that will, one day, engulf us.

Grange-over-Sands

Hail battered the windscreen,
halted my journey, forced
me to think of something
outside the car,
something elemental.

Within minutes
searing sun and promises
so I went ahead
in my small world on wheels.

Next there was rain, grey sea and mist
glimpsed between trees,
there were buildings of slate and stone,
narrow alleys,

two muffled walkers, Lowry figures
leaning into the wind,
then it was the narrow peninsula whose end
slopes sheer off the edge of earth.

I left the car, walked out into winter sun
towards a stretch of shaking sand,
deserted, gleaming, utterly flat,
and miles to lure you forward.

Without the engine, the cage of metal
and everything seen through glass,
ghosts called me to remember where I was,
on the edge of shifting ground
with its layers of bodies underneath.

Dolphins

Not that they came
but that we were there when they did,
a few people scattered on the shore
of the firth holding our breath,

drawn in by shiny wet curves
lifting through the waves,
soaring into air, pirouetting through light,
to plunge and rise again.

Not that they moved
to a secret music - though they did -
but that even in their search
for a kill they gazed at us
as if they knew we were held.

Not that they stayed an hour
then left one by one
in a farewell flourish
but that we knew
we could never signal back.

Great Barrier Reef
A ghazal

Though we had teenage dreams and student plans to swim the reef,
work and mortgages smothered our longing to swim the reef.

We kept our list, Victoria Falls, Grand Canyon, Uluru, and the place
you most wanted to see, Queensland's Great Barrier Reef.

Years later, through curtains of rainforest leaves, we watched youngsters
surfing the waves, and thought ourselves too old to swim the reef.

You only knew a few unconfident strokes and I was worried
you'd be overcome by the swell if you tried to swim the reef,

but we pulled on wetsuits, jumped from the boat and saw blacktip sharks,
butterfly fish, coral streaked with electric blue, the day we swam the reef.

We never knew enough of the earth, never saw tigers or condors,
killer whales or eyeless moles beneath black sand, but we swam the reef.

We didn't build castles, compose sonatas, write bestseller books,
but, while there was still time, at least we swam the reef.

I must let go of grief, remember what we had, the wonders of the Dales,
the slopes of Pen-y-ghent, and that, against the odds, we swam the reef.

Rivers

I thought I saw you
across the Humber

outlined in morning mist
and I walked through

the Land of Green Ginger
down to the water's edge

then the river changed
and I found myself beside the Ribble

where, on the far bank, you seemed
to stand in showers of light

and, even in my dream, I recalled
the times we watched the glint

of salmon who tried to leap
the falls and never made it.

You spoke, but your words were
lost in the pounding of the water.

To my visitor

When you come I hope you will take me
just once more to my favourite places
where once I felt I was most alive:

to climb trees on Healey Heights,
snag our fingers on rough bark, knock down
a hatful of conkers, trapeze through the boughs;

at Wycoller to wade through the stream
catching our breath where waters meet
in a swirl as icy as chilled champagne;

to walk through the ancient Forest of Bowland,
scale the gritstone of Pendle Hill,
look over the edges of deep-cut cloughs;

at Silverdale, to run on the salted beach,
skim polished pebbles, and wait for
the sun to slide slowly into the sea.

And you'll take me to be with Yeoman
again, and I'll climb on his back
and cling to his mane as he takes me
through the woods and off the beaten track

then there'll be Blaze the racehorse
who galloped me to the edge of the cliff.

III

Feral Cat

Feral cat

Out of unpruned bushes
a belly slunk along the ground
and he appeared

intent as a tiger,
bones sticking out like blades,
eyes huge in the cave of his face.

I never cared for cats
and I'm a vegetarian
yet now I buy and chop up
chunks of meat
leave them outside the kitchen door

but, though he comes
almost every day,
he never lets me see him eat.

I feel this creature has chosen me
and have begun to need his slow stealth
stalking my jungle of weeds.

Fashion accessory

She was a handbag dog,
receiver of titbits
from manicured fingers,
and every night lay like a silk scarf
across the velvet of her basket

until that time an autumn moon
threw white light across the walls
and drew her outside
to flashing neon, raucous voices,
music pumped in a bass key.

Almost hit by a roaring bus
she sprawled in the gutter
a mess in oil and dirt.

Then her ears picked up new messages,
her nose took on a life of its own,
she gobbled discarded pizza,
trawled her way along the gutter
and stumbled for miles

until she found again that wash of light
where trees threw deep shadows,
grass and earth soothed her paws,
and only halted when she heard
wolves howling as they came for her.

She rolled over, panting submission,
and slowly became not prey
but a cub in unfamiliar form
and found herself at the heart of a pack
with a seasoned old wolf at its head,
prowling up the hill and over the moor.

All I did

All I did was sleep
in your compost heap

they turfed me out
of the sewers
flushed me out
of the drains

and I had the kids
to think about

my need to find shelter
my need to find food

and you and your kind
think only of dirt
and fear what's in the soil

I'm rotting here
eaten by poison
you paid someone else
to give

and you
you continue
to live your life.

The lions

The lions left their plinths to prowl the midnight
streets. Ignoring traffic lights and yellow lines,
they overturned bins behind darkened shops,
ripped out stunted, urban trees,
carried mice and foxes in their jaws.

The rumour was, their favourite prey
were children who wouldn't eat their greens
or brush their teeth
and sang rude words to the hymns in church.

Kids cowered under their quilts
feeling hot breath and penknife claws,
thinking of their mother's rubber band lips,
the teacher's springy cane,
the voice of the preacher relishing hell.

One night a boy who'd had enough
left his mum and dad to their bedroom noises,
his teddy bear guarding the pillow,
and, prising his window open,
swivelled his legs over the sill
and swung down the drainpipe.

Now, if you dare to go out in the dark
you'll see gangs of children in Tarzan pyjamas
roaming the night, noses twitching, ears pricked.

Overnight

Every morning in the garden
the usual overnight signs:
rummaged leaves in the border,
silver trails along the paths,
upturned soil on the lawn.

But today, the first snow
tells a tale of other creatures
possessing the garden at night:
something with three splayed toes,

something with paw prints
bigger than my hand
and, leaving hardly any white
unbroken, the dark imprints
of hooves.

I want to meet these creatures
and tonight, wrapped in my fleece,
I shall stay awake out here,
curled up like a cat by the open gate.

Stony lane

Every leaf was clear against the sun,
wild scabious held peacock butterflies
and a thrush perched on a hawthorn bush
its throat trembling with song.

So much light, so much warmth,
but I wouldn't stop on the stony lane -
I wanted to outwalk my body
and, breathless, reached the top.

I leant against the limestone
of the stable block whose shutters
were flung wide, and - solid
against the shadows - saw him,
the chestnut horse I often visited.

Near enough for me to feel his breath,
he didn't snort or waterfall his mane,
didn't come snuggling for apples
or to be stroked along the white blaze of his face.

He simply waited and let me be
as I spoke to him, heavy with words,
and the day folded itself around me.

Under the saddle

I've fallen with my head so close
to this huge jagged rock, I can see
its weathered markings as carved symbols
re-telling ancient myths.
It could be one of the erratics, flung
around when these dales were formed.

Above me, the horse stands as still
as if he hadn't just galloped
reckless as a racer, giving me
Whistlejacket, Altisadora,
Red Rum, under the saddle,
and tumbled me into the earth.

Blood seeps through the sleeve
of my torn sweater, several bruises
ache but my limbs seem intact.

The horse rests on delicate-looking
legs, his long head full of history,
Bucephalas, Marengo, back to Pegasus,
to Greece, to Egypt, one of the horses
painted on rock alongside
mysterious hieroglyphs.

Crystal horse

Stella McCartney's chandelier at Belsay Castle is a life-size horse made of over eight thousand crystal spheres.

In the shadows I see ghosts of broken horses,
blind pit ponies, war horses tangled in wire,
and the four prophesied, the white, the red,
the black, the pale horses.

Among them race the wild
Mongolian Przewalskis,
the feral Mustangs, those wild west pioneers,
and the snowy stallions of the Camargue
born of the waves, white tails smoking.

Here, too, in the turret recesses,
gallop Kelpies, centaurs, unicorns.

Horses of myth and history haunt this place
coming and going in the dark spaces of the castle,
and in the foreground, leaping in the light,
forelegs lifted, back legs bent, long tail flowing,
the prancing horse of crystal rain.

Presence

No undergrowth, tangled bushes
or hedges, but in that suburban garden

I saw a Dürer come to life
there on my concrete drive

a baby hare
crouched in stillness,
the curve of his spine haloed
by the sun, his folded limbs
hiding the hinges of his speed,
his long ears alert
and tipped with light.

I held my breath until
he sprang up the apple tree,
froze in the fork of a branch
and waited for the dark.

That night
in my cage of sleep
I dreamt of hares in the wild
and, when I woke, wanted
without any trappings
simply to be.

The Egyptian hieroglyph of a hare depicts the verb 'to be'.

Unsuitable shoes

At the top of the promenade steps
halfway between home and the edge
of the sea, the day turns from light
and sun to sullen rain. My socks
weep in my unsuitable shoes.

The steps are steep and winding,
tricky bends hide what lies ahead.
Wet seaweed and mud clog the stone,
crumbling edges drip green slime.

A dog, a curly-haired caramel dog,
looks at the steps with eager eyes,
tail wagging like a breezy pennant.

He stops to let me go first. Imagining
broken bones and overstretched lungs,
I hesitate and, besides,
something might happen here.

A train might canter across the bay
a horse appear trailing smoke
an angel step down from a tree.

But there's no-one and nothing
except silence and this gap in the day.
And already the caramel dog
has had another minute of joy.

Drama school

Drama schools are fond of sending students
to the zoo to study the behaviour of beasts.
It's what people laugh at when they speak about
the 'luvvies': be a cat, be a dog, be a bloody giraffe.

But look, Lear's on his knees and clawing Cordelia.
His hands are paws and he's mauling her body
round the stage, frantic to revive her.

He's done the mad scene in the storm
railed against every roof
cried: Never, never, never, never, never.

Now he makes us see what we all are
at heart: animals learning to grieve.

Wild

Nothing, no-one, until he came down
from the high fields and wove his way
like a dark thread stitching the mist,
his voice echoing from rock to rock.

In the haze he had little substance.
I longed for something the eye could grasp
yet I knew he was a gift returning
though with edges like a sword.

He moved towards me, this creature
I knew long ago, then stopped as if tethered
and hung his head waiting for me to call.
I knew if I didn't he'd be gone forever.

I stepped forward and whispered his name.
He shook himself free, bucked and kicked
against the wind, came and restored
in me the dark, the daring, the wild.

The twinning of books

In bed
I'm reading *Being Mortal*
and my lavatory book
is *Feral*.

Behind my back
they've knitted together
like two-ply wool
and there's no untangling them.

Being mortal's a terrible thing,
a mountain steeper than Everest,
mysterious as Fuji.

The one is a struggle
with lack of air, weakness of limbs,
thickening of arteries.
The other wants to touch your soul.

Feral's a plea
for freedom to have an affair
with the earth

to go down to the roots of oaks,
into the deepest blue of gentians,
to plunge in icy rivers under
the waterfall's thrashing beat,

to shout into the wind
expecting no answer
to being mortal,
being feral.

IV

Speak to the Earth

Garsdale

Now I find it's a hard walk
to the waterfall over stubbly, marshy land
but I still long to see
the early light on the river.

I still long to see massed foxgloves,
wild scabious, woodland geraniums
flaunting stamens, pistils, pollen,
feel under my toes the grass velvet with moss

rub my fingers against the rough
bark of the giant beeches
be close enough to smell the wild roses
where bees search for nectar.

I want to taste the rain and sun
grown into fat pods and fruit
be one with the flourishing earth.

If it happens

If the beaver returns to the water,
to its tasks of felling and damming,

wild ponies and foxes are left alone,
badgers, boar and cattle find their place again

and pheasants don't need to fear
the guns. If the lynx at night

shows hunting eyes, if wolves
cull the needed number of deer,

and a careless grace returns
to everything, even to death,

and life and death recover their rhythm,
what will it be like to dare

everything, to be one with the flesh
and blood that makes the earth?

Put an ear to the ground

Put an ear to the ground
listen for the code
of hooves drumming
across the surface,
the rustle of grasses,
mumble of insects

the roar of fire
at the molten centre,
rumble of fault lines,
wind echoing in limestone caves,
drip of water carving them out.

Your ears reach for fainter messages
you can't quite hear,
earth conducting its business
with no need whatever of you.

Gagudju man
Remembering Bill Neidjie ('I'm telling you this while you've got time')

This was the man who shared
the long-held secrets of his world.
I met him in Alice Springs, sat with him
in the aboriginal silence, knowing
his closeness to every living thing.

He felt trees in his body,
their trunks and leaves pumping water
as human hearts pump blood,
thought that no matter what kind -
kangaroo, eagle, echidna -
animals pulse in our flesh,

said, if you harm what is sacred,
you might get a cyclone or flood,
or kill someone in another place,
told us we must hang on to the land,
the trees, the soil, because of the day
when we become the earth.

Madeleine

She hates crowds, noise,
shops, so we go into the wild,
not a word exchanged.

We've seen young foxes at play,
untamed ponies roaming the moor,
deer browsing the trees,
and today lie on our backs
loving the glide of red kites
in the air above.

She hurls herself off the branch of a tree,
squelches her feet in mud,
runs, flops, jumps, zooms, races
with arms flung wide like wings.

Those with their stethoscopes,
case notes and pens
want her to sit at a desk,
to use pedestrian crossings,
and her mother's bone-tired
trying to get her to infants' school.

But today we forget
the dark, the sleepless nights,
the nervous system on edge

for Maddie's in touch
with the earth,
Maddie is running free.

And if, after all

there's nothing left
on this blue planet
after we've had our way
if, in our dreams,
we replenish it

bring back the trees,
root them more firmly,
let rivers choose their
winding course, and only
beavers interfere, add nothing
poisonous to earth,

let the seas teach us
where power lies,
let horses, sheep and cattle
couple when they choose,

might humankind once more
live with miracles
and might I learn
to walk naked again?

Beech tree

After a hundred years of growing, I felt
a knife gouge doggedly into me, dragging
this way and that, creak, crack, carving
the corners of each letter. This man, wanting
people to read him in the flesh of a tree,
pierced me till the sap ran, and for years
I've been forming scabs, re-shaping every
word, lumpy as stitches left in a wound.

Today, passers-by can still see this was Steve,
but his surname's unguessable now
and the date reads nineteen-ninety-squiggle
where his life has grown into mine.

Kindling

A small chunk of firewood,
yet it has layer upon layer
of beech and bark

layer upon layer of years
revealed by the axe.

If left to nature,
ages later it would be found
pressed into the earth
and might be diamond or coal

or, before the axe,
would still be part of a full-height tree
with branch and leaf rippling
the light and casting shade

and, earlier still, a beech standing
a mere twelve feet, or ten or five

or a fresh green sapling
feeding on the death of leaves
dropped decades ago.

Wild rhododendrons

Some sleight of hand shifted the air,
called us from the familiar lane
with shades of purple, white and pink.
We pushed through knee-high grass
our toes stumbling in roots of blackberry,
pitfalled earth threatened our ankles,
thorns drew blood, nettles and thistles
spread rashes on our bare skin.

It was as if an ancient god had lifted acres
of parkland high over the stony hills
and dropped them in a forgotten place
to run wild. We found ourselves within circles
of bloom where sunlight waterfalled
through the leaves and the bushes seemed to burn.

We'd left all we knew and reached
that place where the murmurs of earth
turn to music. And all the answers
lay just beyond our fingertips.

In praise of the potato

Secretly growing for months
buried in earth, it already
has a cluster of eyes to give life
to a new generation.

My fork presses a freckling
of tiny holes and there's a squish
of moisture, a faint smell of muck
and grass, then I apply heat

and wait, remembering so many
before, fished from the hot ashes
of Guy Fawkes nights as the sky
filled with detonating rainbows
and laughing people
burned their eager mouths.

Out of the oven, red hot,
steam breathing out
of a crisply cracking jacket.
Flesh yields to oozing butter,
blends to a thick cream,

bliss in a mouthful, food of the gods,
staple for millions, spread from Peru
across the earth. Give thanks to Axomamma
for Russet Burbank, Nishiyutaka,
Cranberry Red, Amorosa, and Yukon Gold.

Axomamma: in Inca mythology, the goddess of potatoes.

Restless land

I wake from the peaks and troughs of night
in a house teetering on the edge
of a sheer valley sliced out by a giant axe
swung by a woodsman from Nordic myth.

Today the stillness is complete,
massed hawthorns squat on the top
and along the valley sides
interwoven with gorse and grasses
that reach for a hold on plunging sides
like soldiers digging in.

The sun's too hot for December.
I had expected and wanted greyness,
wilderness, storm.

The buildings, unpolished slate
and stone quarried long ago
have their share of history
and of sorrow, and the roots
of this house have been known
to move in the shriek and lash of wind,
the heave of restless land.

The path of desire

The path of desire is the path
they don't want me to take.

What they want for me is tarmac, fences,
gates, the watchful eyes of street lamps.

They don't want me to know the roughness
of rock-littered lanes, the excitement of snow and ice.

They don't want me to walk out of range;
will call me back, put a leash on me.

They'd rather I never stepped outside
but stayed shut in by walls

in a world as soft as stuffed armchairs,
my only landscape on TV.

I know my destination and that I want to get there
along the worn earth of the bootleg trail.

A path of desire or a bootleg trail is a walking path or track worn into the ground by habitual human passage rather than by design.

V

Legacy

The strangers

They came over the hill as if
we were the strangers. Their feet
were bare and toughened
their bodies smeared with paint
and they carried spears and clubs.

Nearer and nearer they came.
We were too mesmerised
to move even when
we saw the grimness in their eyes,
the fierceness in their lips.

Our breath shortened,
our limbs trembled, but
something in us knew that
they had to come: we recognised
their title to this land.

Gaia writes home

I'm boiling over to tell you
in the beginning was Chaos, vast and dark
it's vastly worse than I feared
then Gaia, deep-breasted earth, was born
my children have turned swords against me
there was light
night and day
destroyed the rhythms
night was crowned with stars
in the arc of heaven
chaos is hurtling back
mountains were worshipped
snow-capped crests are dumping grounds
seas curled fresh upon the shore
there's plastic, strangled seals, poisoned fish
rivers ran and rain refreshed
drought, fire, collapsing ice, floods,
the wiping out of animals and plants.
I thought to hurl lightning thunderbolts
to drop fire and pestilence on their heads
but they're doing all that themselves.

Cross-questioning

Earth laid waste, trashed beyond saving?
Well, you've made a big mistake. I've done nothing.

You should be out looking for vandals,
kids on asbos, thieves, all those people

who aren't me. Thousands dying?
You can't pin that one on me.

Go after the usual suspects, thugs
with a record, youths in hoodies.

Evidence? Footprints? Why pick on me?
It could be a whole group of people

and I swear I've never been near a gang.
I'm respectable. Not even a parking fine.

What was that about a solicitor?
No comment. No comment. No comment.

Waking

I wake to bed linen strewn
around like manic laundry
and can't get out of my head
the creatures I dreamt of
who eat only fruit and leaves

and gaze at the beings
who hack down trees, ravage
land, sea and air, blast their kind
off the earth, and bring silence,
the silence of the animals.

On my way to meet the morning
I'm desperate to hear the bleating
of sheep, the trill of blackbirds,
a dog barking after a stick,
but nothing moves, nothing speaks.

Ice storm

Louder than the roar of the wrecking gales,
crash after crash.

Missiles hit so hard
I thought windows had smashed
or hurtled out of their frames
doors disintegrated to splinters.

Trapped in a flimsy now believably temporary house
I feared if I went outside I'd bleed.

Sheets of ice rained down, hit the ground,
smashed into sharp slices that, lifted by the whirlwind,
attacked everything in their path
as more frozen chunks dropped, cracked, flew.

I thought of the Arctic and the breaking ice
as my small world shook around me.

The dogs

The dogs feel the rub of the collar and the choke-chain
pulled tight. The dogs feel the leash used as a whip.
The dogs feel their hollow bellies, protruding ribs.
The dogs feel their skin grow scabby, infested with fleas.

The dogs feel the kicks that turf them out.
The dogs hate the kennels they're shoved in.
The dogs fear the midnight yards where they're
beaten daily to teach them the hate in snarling.

The tamed dogs play on their owners' weakness
these dogs have learned the art of waiting.
Every eye to melt your heart hides calculation
every *sit up and beg* a shit-load of contempt.

The dogs with docked tails are growing them back.
The dogs with the caved-in lungs approved by Crufts
have learned to breathe again and the dogs with their
bred-out stunted legs are standing tall once more.

The dogs have learned a watchful patience.
The dogs try the length of their leash, know it to an inch.
The dogs are gobbling lumps of meat and grain
preparing to hurl the world back into the wild.

Under their silly haircuts, under their strangled fur,
the wolf in them stirs and starts to grow.
Now in touch with each other, they are
howling in the night, howling across continents.

Tyger

Be afraid.
I live
in the shadows.

You like to think you know me
from specious art
and sanitised safaris

but you should know
that when I hunt
I'm ruthless
so swift
you hardly see me.

I kill to live
and your words about me
are feeble in the extreme.

If I'm wounded
or hungry for too long,
I'll stalk you and other men.

I'm patient and will quietly
track you for hours or lie in wait
downwind

then grab you from behind
or on your blind side
bite you and maul you
till you bleed to death.

But I'm not careless
I don't trash things
don't destroy what I walk on
can smell the approach
of fire, or danger from man.

Be afraid.
I live in the shadows
waiting.

Palm Cove, Queensland

I jerk awake from a nap on the sand
to find the sea is boiling, the beach
has turned to concrete, the sky is red.
I want to backtrack, find the landscape,
the trees that will surely prove
all this is a nightmare.

I dash from place to place,
but no matter which direction I take,
towards the heat, away from the heat,
to the east, to the west, I stub
my toes on cracked barren ground.
Somewhere there have to be trees -

after all, I came straight from
the rainforest bordering the sands -
there have to be vast trunks, leaves,
shade, there have to be crimson rosellas,
thornbills, sulphur crested cockatoos,
there have to be weeds.

Legacy
(to my grandchildren)

For you I wanted to keep a hoard
of green stroked by the breeze,
a sky criss-crossed by birds,

but now I know you might never
encounter wilderness, dig your fingers
into earth, splash in waterfalls,
see dolphins, lions, tigers.

You might have a link
to what once was wild if urban foxes
still survive on scraps of food
from plastic bins.

We failed in the end with every camp,
didn't shout loud enough about war,
were wearied with kettled marches
and the fight to save the trees.

Now my only legacy
is shit and debris,
these few words, and love
that's no longer enough.

Naked Eye Publishing
A fresh approach

Naked Eye Publishing is a completely new outfit, four years in existence and still fledgling: an independent not-for-profit micro-press intent on publishing quality poetry and literature, including in translation. We are also developing a 'Potted Theses' series: academic theses rewritten for the general reader.

A particular focus is translation. We aim to take a midwife role in facilitating the translation of works that have until now been disregarded by English-language publishing. We will be happy if we function purely as an initial stepping-stone both for overlooked writers and first-time literary translators.

Each of us at Naked Eye is a volunteer, competent and professional in our work practice, and not intending to make a profit for the press. We see ourselves as part of the revolution in book publishing, embodying the newly levelled playing field, sidestepping the publishing establishment to produce beautiful books at an affordable price.

nakedeyepublishing.co.uk

www.ingramcontent.com/pod-product-compliance
Lightning Source LLC
Chambersburg PA
CBHW071317080526
44587CB00018B/3261